Will You Marry Me?

THE WORLD'S MOST ROMANTIC PROPOSALS

Cynthia Clumeck Muchnick

Macmillan•USA

Macmillan General Reference
A Simon & Schuster Macmillan Company
1633 Broadway
New York, NY 10019-6785

Library of Congress Cataloging-in-Publication Data
Muchnick, Cynthia Clumeck.
Will you marry me? : the world's most romantic proposals / Cynthia
Clumeck Muchnick.
p. cm.
ISBN: 0-02-861048-2
1. Marriage proposals. I. Title.
GT2650.M83 1996
392'.4—dc20 95-42924
CIP
Book design by Anne Scatto / PIXEL PRESS
Drawings by Jacki Gelb
Manufactured in the United States of America
10 9 8 7 6 5 4 3 2

Contents

Preface * vii

My Storybook Proposal * ix

Athletic Proposals * 1

Beach Proposals * 5

Cyberspace Proposals * 9

Dining Proposals * 13

Elegant Proposals * 17

First-Date Proposals * 21

Game Proposals * 25

High-Flying Proposals ✲ 29

Innovative Proposals ✲ 33

Jumping Proposals ✲ 37

Kind-of-Silly Proposals ✲ 41

Landmark Proposals ✲ 47

Movie Proposals ✲ 51

No-Holds-Barred Proposals ✲ 55

On-the-Job Proposals ✲ 59

Picnic Proposals ✲ 65

Quirky Proposals ✲ 69

Romantic Proposals ✲ 75

Second-Time-Around Proposals ✲ 79

TV Proposals * 83

Underwater Proposals * 87

Vacation Proposals * 91

Women's Proposals to Men * 95

X-Rated Proposals * 99

Yuppie Proposals * 103

Zany Proposals * 107

Concluding Remarks * 113

About the Author * 115

Send Me Your Marriage Proposals! * 116

Acknowledgments * 117

For Adam, for asking.

Preface

. . . And Prince Charming got down on his knee and proposed to the princess. Then the lovers rode off on his white stallion into the sunset and lived happily ever after.

What's your idea of the perfect proposal? If you're as romantic as I am, you probably imagined that special moment way back when you were a child, long before there was a real Prince Charming in your life. In *Will You Marry Me?* more than fifty newlywed couples share their precious memories of the magical moment they decided to wed.

Because a marriage proposal is such a special event, its story is likely to be told and retold for years to come. When I became engaged, the first question I heard from family and friends was "How did he pop the question?" Since my husband was clever enough to engineer an incredible storybook proposal, I always enjoy the opportunity to retell—and relive—the memory of my engagement.

In retelling my story, I learned that other friends and relatives had also experienced fairy tale proposals, ones that meant as much to them as mine did to me. These proposals came in all shapes and sizes. They ranged from very public declarations of love spelled out on a football scoreboard to strictly private love notes scratched in the sand on a secluded beach to whispered confidences made high above the earth in a hot-air balloon. Not only were the locations significant, but so were the ways in which each proposal was made.

Will You Marry Me? captures the magic and romance of these memorable proposals. Collected from couples all across America, these stories run the gamut from the classic to the outrageous. They are arranged from A (Athletic) to Z (Zany) to present an alphabet of "engaging" anecdotes that can serve as the inspiration for your own perfect proposal.

My Storybook Proposal

*O*ur first kiss was at the Rodin Sculpture Garden, the romantic spot on our college campus at Stanford University. Less than three years later, on a spring break vacation, Adam and I visited the Rodin Sculpture Garden in Paris. Having studied art history in college, I was thrilled to be with my boyfriend in this most perfect setting. After a romantic stroll through the garden, we sat down on a park bench for a friendly game of Scrabble.™ (We are Scrabble buffs, and our Travel Scrabble game accompanies us everywhere!) As the game progressed, Adam managed to filch some tiles from the bag, and he placed them on the board. When he put down the word "MARRY," I giggled nervously, finding it odd that he should make such a strategically bad move and give me a chance for a Triple Word Score.

Then he asked me, "What do you see?"

"What do I see?" I echoed.

Adam got down on one knee, pulled a ring out of his blue jeans' pocket, and pointed to the words scattered on the board: "WILL... YOU... MARRY... ME"?

I was numb, shocked, excited, overwhelmed. I couldn't reply....

He repeated, "I am asking you to be my wife. Will you?"

That was my cue. "YES! Of course I will marry you!"

What a blissful moment, frozen in my memory like a perfect photographic image. We hugged. We kissed. We called our families from a phone booth on the corner. This was the beginning of our happily ever after.

❧

What is it that made such an impression on me and spurred me to write this book? It was my husband's care and attention to every detail of making this special moment so unforgettable. He combined the romance of Paris, the creativity of asking me with the lettered tiles of our favorite game, and the symbolism of proposing in the Parisian counterpart of the spot where we first kissed in college. The moment that we decided to become teammates for life was so perfect that I had to share it with other lovers everywhere.

$\mathcal{A}$ IS FOR
ATHLETIC PROPOSALS

You have all seen the planes that hover over sports stadiums trailing messages that read: "Sherri, just say yes!" or "Ron, will you marry me?" Maybe you've even seen the magic question appear in lights on the scoreboard at half time. One enthusiastic fiancé-to-be actually arranged to throw the first pitch at a ball game and have the catcher present his girlfriend with the ring. Talk about throwing her a curve ball! Thank goodness she said yes and he didn't strike out! Then there was the tennis player who took advantage of a score of forty—love to get down on his knee and ask his partner to make it forever love. Whatever the athletic twist may be, if you are a couple who enjoy watching or participating in sporting events together, an athletic approach to your proposal is sure be a winner.

.... ❧ ....

𝓜ike and Rachel met on the track team in college. Mike had spent several months training for the New York City Marathon, and when he finally crossed the finish line Rachel was there to greet him with open arms. She never imagined, however, that Mike had been carrying an engagement ring in the Velcro coin purse attached to his sneaker laces for the entire twenty-six miles. Instead of falling to the ground in exhaustion, Mike got down on one knee, pulled out the ring, and popped the question. Rachel hugged his hot, sweaty body, laughing and crying at once, and their relationship was off to a running start.

❧

$\mathcal{T}$im took Pam to an unusual place for dinner: St. Louis's Busch stadium. A special table was set up on the pitcher's mound for a candlelight dinner. Tim had arranged for a violinist to serenade them and a tuxedoed waiter to serve the elegant meal, which had been ordered from their favorite restaurant. As the enchanted evening drew to a close, Tim asked Pam to be his teammate for life. When Pam replied "Yes," the scoreboard flashed, "HOME RUN!!!"

❧

The seventh-inning stretch is a popular time to spring the big question. Sean added a twist to this event by getting the stadium cameraman to zoom in on him and his girlfriend, Tess, and displaying his proposal on the Diamond Vision screen. As the P.A. system played "Take Me Out to the Ball Game," Sean produced a box of Crackerjacks that contained an engagement ring as a prize!

$\mathcal{B}$ IS FOR
BEACH PROPOSALS

There's no more romantic spot for a proposal than the beach at sunset. After a delightful day spent building sand castles and collecting seashells, what could be more thrilling than finding a sparkling engagement ring at the bottom of an exotic drink served in a coconut? Or how about fishing together off a pier and, while her head is turned, attaching a fake ring to her fish hook so that she reels in a catch unlike any other? Then, too, there's always the possibility of stumbling upon a strategically placed bottle containing a clue to the whereabouts of a very special ring. Just be careful not to get too close to the ocean when you place the ring on her finger, for if you drop it, your romantic moment could be washed away!

.... ❧ ....

*M*arc and Kim were walking hand-in-hand on a nearly deserted beach one balmy evening. When they came upon a smooth patch of sand, Marc picked up a stick and scratched out the words, "Kimmy, will you marry me?" She thought he was kidding, until he took an engagement ring off his neck chain. Since Kim hadn't noticed the ring the entire time they were walking along the beach, Marc finally decided to spell out his message for her. That got Kim's attention—and a resounding "Yes!"

❧

$\mathcal{S}$teven planned the perfect get-away beach proposal. He surprised Debby with a trip to a tropical paradise in the Caribbean. This tiny, upscale Gilligan's Island, complete with thatched-hut suites, outdoor showers, and hot tubs, was just the spot for a romantic rendezvous. Upon their arrival, Steven was forced to postpone his sunset proposal because of a sudden tropical storm. Determined not to let Mother Nature stifle his plans, he waited until day two, and as the sun set on a quiet beach, he got down on one knee and popped the question. Certainly, this relationship will be able to weather many a storm.

✤

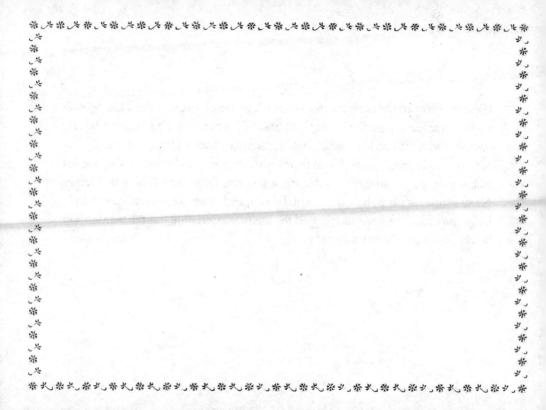

$\mathcal{C}$ IS FOR
CYBERSPACE PROPOSALS

Cyberspace can prove to be as romantic a location as a moonlit beach or a candlelit restaurant. By using a modem and logging onto the World Wide Web, you, too, may meet the man or woman of your wildest dreams.

$\mathscr{M}$ax and Jody met on the Internet, and their communications in cyberspace led to a whirlwind romance. They "spoke" at least three times a day via computer and always looked forward to their next chat. Eventually, they progressed from computer chats to phone chats to face-to-face chats.

As their relationship deepened they shared many intimate lifetime goals and dreams. Then one night Max surprised Jody by blurting out over the Internet: WILL YOU MARRY ME? Jody's response was "Yse!" Although Jody in her excitement had jumbled her typed letters, Max saw through the typo and now these two have formed a permanent network connection.

$\mathcal{D}$ennis met Liz at the gym through mutual friends. They started dating and spent so much time on the phone to each other during the work day that both were reprimanded for their costly toll calls. Searching for a more discreet form of communication, they switched to E-mail. They developed all sorts of cute "code words" such as " :)" for a "happy face" and "——>" for "see you later." They both spent the majority of their lunch hours in E-mail conversation until one day, Dennis typed: "Liz, you're the first person I want to talk to every day and the last person I want to see at night. I love working out together at the end of each day and spending my waking hours daydreaming of you. Why not save ourselves some rent money and stop tying up the Internet and just become husband and wife? I love you, Lizzy, and want to be your partner for life. What do you say?"

Liz responded, ":):):):):):):):):):)YYYYYEEEEESSSSS:):):):):):):):):):)!!!!"

Many E-mail conversations followed as they planned for their wedding and the start of their journey together down the superhighway of life.

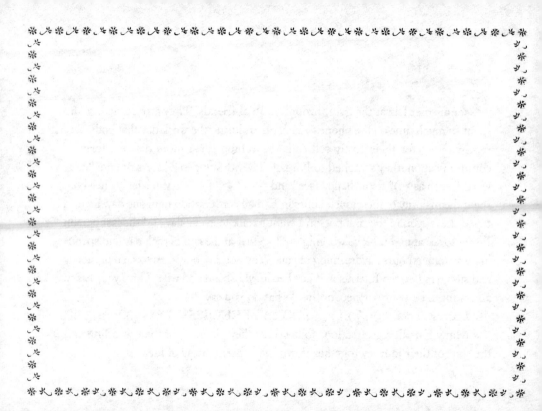

$\mathcal{D}$ IS FOR
DINING PROPOSALS

Soft music, good wine, candlelight, a cozy fireplace in a romantic restaurant, and a couple in love. What more could you ask to set the mood for a memorable proposal?

$\mathcal{G}$reg and Celeste became engaged over lunch. He took her to a charming country inn and arranged to be called to the phone before the salad was served. Instead of answering the phone, though, Greg slipped into the kitchen, and hid a black velvet box at the bottom of the salad bowl intended for Celeste. Greg returned to the table just as the salad course was being served.

Celeste began to eat. On her second bite, her fork poked something hard. When she pushed the lettuce aside and noticed something black, she screamed, "There's a bug in my salad!" Greg used a spoon to lift out the box now drenched in vinaigrette dressing. He then opened the box to reveal a beautiful ring and punned to Celeste, "Lettuce live happily ever after."

$\mathcal{O}$n Tracy's birthday, Bobby took her to their favorite restaurant in New York City. Along with the dessert and champagne, Bobby presented Tracy with a large, beautifully wrapped gift. Tracy eagerly opened the box only to find it contained a sweatshirt from Stanford, Bobby's alma mater. She had been hoping for something slightly more sentimental, but she did not want to show her disappointment, so she thanked Bobby and started to take the sweatshirt out of the box. As she did so, out fell a small black box. This was the gift Tracy had been longing for. Bobby said the magic words, "Will you marry me?" and Tracy deemed her birthday a five-star dining experience.

P.S. One word of warning: NEVER let the ring out of your sight. Do not entrust it to a waiter or a bus boy or a hostess to be presented later in the evening, for you may be surprised to find that your accomplice has disappeared along with your expensive ring.

E IS FOR
ELEGANT PROPOSALS

An elegant ambiance can make any proposal more romantic. Even a simple picnic can become an elegant affair with the addition of a colorful tablecloth set with china and crystal and a vase full of fresh flowers.

$\mathcal{J}$onathan surprised Caren with a romantic dinner at a very special restaurant where couples dine in secluded private booths. Jonathan arranged for a cozy banquette on a balcony overlooking the city below, and he pre-ordered an exquisite seven-course meal, complete with tiny scoops of sherbet served between courses to cleanse their palettes. At the end of the meal, the white-gloved waiter set a black plate with a silver dome over it in the center of the table. When he lifted the cover, Caren couldn't believe her eyes. There on the black plate were the words "Will you marry me?" artfully drizzled in white chocolate. Around this message was a mouthwatering array of candy flowers and tiny sweet confections. To top off this scrumptious proposal, Jonathan serenaded Caren with a soft and sweet rendition of "Love Me Tender," their song.

✤

$\mathcal{E}$ric invited Adrienne for an elegant dinner at his place to celebrate the first anniversary of their relationship. They had decided to dress up for the occasion and Adrienne arrived ready to celebrate. Much to her surprise, Adrienne was greeted at the door by a white-gloved butler who took her coat and ushered her into Eric's living room. Eric had been cooking all day and he had hired the butler to add an elegant touch to their evening. Hors d'oeuvres and champagne arrived on a silver tray, and Eric proposed a toast, "To our wonderful first year together, a bright future and many years of happiness." As Adrienne removed her glass from the tray, she noticed her name engraved on it. She looked closer and saw more than her name on the tray. The message she saw was this: "Adrienne, I love you. Will you marry me?" Now that qualifies as love served up on a silver platter!

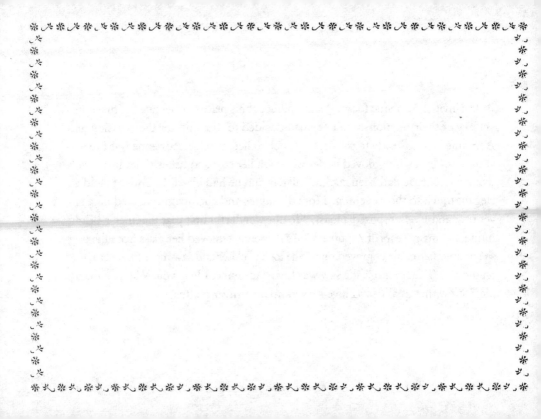

$\mathcal{F}$ IS FOR
FIRST-DATE PROPOSALS

No, there have not yet been any verified stories of marriage proposals on a first date. Many people, however, have returned to the scene of their first date to pop the magic question.

$\mathcal{L}$ouise and Ivan spent their first date skating arm-in-arm at the Rockefeller Center ice rink in New York City. Because they enjoyed skating together, they returned to the ice rink several times, but one time Ivan arranged a special treat for Louise. When the DJ requested that everyone clear the ice, Ivan took Louise by the hand and skated to the center of the rink. Suddenly, a spotlight shone down on the couple and their song, "No Ordinary Love," began to play over the loudspeaker. Struggling to keep his balance, Ivan got down on one knee and proposed to Louise. He was so nervous that he asked her, "Will you marry *you*?" Louise knew what he meant, though, and she answered, "Yes!" before he had a chance to get cold feet.

*C*indy and Scott met during their student days at Tufts, and they first kissed at a college formal there. Years later, Scott planned the perfect proposal at the same hotel where the formal had been held. He told Cindy that his uncle, a prominent economist, was receiving an honorary award in Boston and the two of them would be joining the rest of his family to celebrate this happy occasion. He then prevailed upon his mother to call Cindy to discuss what they would wear to the event.

Scott and Cindy arrived in Boston early so that they could spend the day at Tufts, revisiting all of the places where they had shared so many happy memories. When they checked in at the hotel, Cindy recalled that this had been the site of their college formal a few years earlier. The desk clerk handed Scott a message from his parents, suggesting that they should all meet in the grand ballroom at 7:00 P.M.

Scott and Cindy dressed for the evening and just as they were ready to head to the festivities, Scott called Cindy over to the window to admire the view from their twenty-ninth floor suite. There at the window he told Cindy how much he loved her and asked her to be his wife. Then he admitted that there was no event in the ballroom. Scott and his mother had set Cindy up for the surprise. He wanted the spot where they had shared their first kiss to be the spot where they agreed to share their lives. I wonder how many more firsts Cindy and Scott will commemorate at this particular hotel?

G IS FOR
GAME PROPOSALS

If you're ready to get out of "The Dating Game" and make a "Love Connection," the toy store offers a host of playful ways to pop the question. Consider making Scrabble,™ charades, Twister,™ Pictionary,™ or even Go Fish part of the gameplan for your proposal and you're sure to come out a winner!

$\mathcal{D}$an and Meredith are addicted to crossword puzzles. In fact, they devote every Sunday morning to doing the crossword that appears in the *New York Times Magazine*. Meredith reads the clues, and Dan ponders the answers. One Sunday, Dan had a surprise planned for his sweetheart. He had worked with a friend who was a computer whiz to design a crossword of his own. In it, he included references to events from their relationship such as:

1 Across   Dan and Meredith's favorite restaurant

5 Down   Dan's favorite flavor of ice cream.

The personalized puzzle appeared miraculously in one Sunday's *New York Times Magazine*. As Meredith filled in the puzzle, she laughed at Dan's imaginative idea, but she never guessed that four of the clues would result in the words: "WILL YOU MARRY ME?" When she came to the final clue of the puzzle, the instruction read: "Combine six across, four down, twenty across, and seventeen down." The sum of these answers added up to the magic question, and Meredith squealed with happiness! She had no "cross words" for this happy occasion.

❧

$\mathscr{K}$evin engineered a cute twist on the crossword puzzle theme when he proposed to Sarah. Flipping to the puzzle in the magazine section one Sunday morning, Sarah found that Kevin had already filled in thirty across to read, "WILL YOU MARRY ME?"

❧

$\mathcal{E}$laine and Spencer were playing a heated game of Monopoly.™ The colored paper money was piled high on both sides. Spencer had hotels on Park Place and the Boardwalk, and Elaine owned all the railroads and electric companies. Spencer collected $200 for passing "Go," when Elaine rolled the dice and landed on a "Chance?" square. She drew the orange card, which read, "Take a risk on me. Do not pass Go. Do not collect $200. Go directly to my heart. You will have free parking for life and I'll keep you out of jail. Will you marry me, Elaine?" Of course, she said, "Yes!" Who could resist a proposal so full of fun and games?

$\mathcal{H}$ IS FOR
HIGH-FLYING PROPOSALS

Romance really takes off with a high-flying proposal made in an airplane or even a hot-air balloon. Such relationships will undoubtedly defy gravity!

$\mathscr{F}$elice and David were headed for David's home for the holidays. They sat together as the plane took off, admiring the view below. Some time later David excused himself to get a magazine, but that's not what he did at all. Instead, he spoke with the flight attendant to plan his surprise proposal. As they were served beverages, the captain announced over the P.A. system, "Ladies and gentlemen, welcome aboard. We are cruising at an altitude of 32,000 feet and we expect a smooth ride. Also, the gentleman in seat 24A would like the lady in seat 24B to marry him!" All of the passengers cheered. The flight attendant returned with a complimentary bottle of champagne and David reached for the motion sickness bag. No, he wasn't feeling ill. He had used the bag to hide Felice's ring. Fortunately there was no turbulence on this flight!

❖

$\mathcal{B}$rad and Jessica had plans to go hot-air ballooning on Valentine's Day. As they floated into the sky, Jessica enjoyed the view. After about fifteen minutes Brad pointed out an old farmhouse below. As the balloon passed over the house, Jessica made out the words painted on the barn roof: "Jess, will you marry me?" She couldn't believe it! Brad broke out a bottle of champagne, and they celebrated a relationship that had reached new heights!

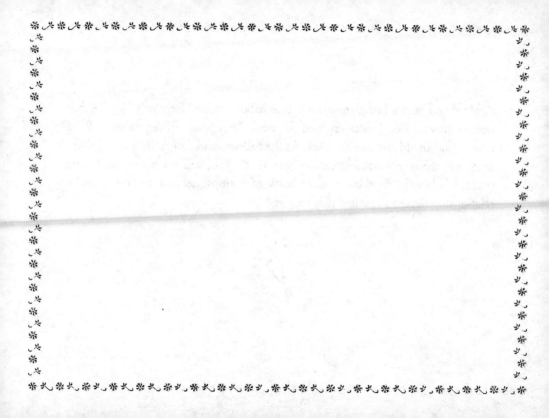

$\mathcal{I}$ IS FOR
INNOVATIVE PROPOSALS

You don't have to be a Thomas Edison to invent your perfect proposal. Just unleash your imagination and you'll be surprised at the unforgettable moment you can come up with.

$\mathcal{J}$eff planned an innovative proposal for Christine. Early one Saturday morning they set off for a golf game at a brand new course, the E. Gadison, located near Chicago's O'Hare Airport.

"E. Gadison, what an odd name for a course!" said Christine.

Jeff just shrugged and kept on driving until they reached the remote airport parking lot.

Christine worried that she would have to carry her heavy golf bag a long distance to the clubhouse. Jeff opened the trunk to get their clubs and took out a piece of cardboard on which he had written EGADISON, the "name" of the golf course. Knowing that Christine loved to play word games, Jeff told her to unscramble the letters. When she did, she realized that the letters spelled: SAN DIEGO, Christine's favorite vacation spot. Jeff had packed clothes for each of them, and from his pocket he produced two plane tickets for sunny southern California.

They arrived at the Hotel Del Coronado, San Diego's historic landmark hotel, just in time to catch the spectacular Pacific sunset. As they walked along the beach, sipping wine and admiring their surroundings, Christine knew that this would be the ideal moment for a marriage proposal, so she stopped and told Jeff that this was the *most beautiful* spot in the world and that she loved him very much. Jeff, though, did not pick up on her cue. He simply smiled pleasantly and continued walking. Moments later, Christine stopped again, giving Jeff another opportunity to pop the question. To her dismay, he didn't. Finally, just as the setting sun reached the horizon, Jeff made his move. He got down on his knee, declared his love for Christine, and asked for her hand in marriage. She accepted, of course, and the two anticipate a lifetime full of innovative surprises and unexpected adventures.

❧

*J*ake awaited the arrival of flight 247 from Omaha, Nebraska. Stephanie, his long-time girlfriend, was coming to town for a visit. Jake arrived at the gate one hour early to prepare for his romantic proposal. He gave to each person at the gate a white rose and a picture of Stephanie. When Stephanie emerged from the plane, fifty strangers handed her white roses one by one. Bewildered, she looked around anxiously for Jake, who was hiding nearby. Once her arms were full of flowers, he appeared, ring in hand, and professed his love to her. Jake's floral tribute marked the beginning of a rosy future for this happy couple.

$\mathcal{J}$ IS FOR
JUMPING PROPOSALS

Propose a leap into the future . . .

Skydiving was a passion for both Matt and Keri. On one outing, just as they were about to jump, Matt popped the question. Delighted, they floated down to earth together on their personal cloud nine.

$\mathcal{L}$indsay and Charley met while taking hang-gliding lessons. After going out for two years, they decided it was time for them to take the real plunge: bungee jumping. On her birthday, Charley treated Lindsay to a bungee jump, which provided not only the perfect birthday gift for Lindsay but also the ideal setting for an unforgettable marriage proposal.

The daring duo eagerly awaited their jumps. Charley was to go first. Just before he jumped from a 150-foot bridge, he handed Lindsay a small red velvet box with a note and asked her to read it once he had jumped. The note read: "To my high-flying gal. Our love knows no boundaries. You are my soul mate and my partner in life's adventures. Please say you'll always be mine. Now open the box." Inside was a gorgeous engagement ring which Lindsay placed on her finger. As she took her jump, she hollered, "YESSSSSSSS!!!" and Charley knew that there was no need to jump-start this engagement!

$\mathscr{K}$ IS FOR
KIND-OF-SILLY PROPOSALS

If you can't take a joke, read no further. If you want to start your future having fun together, here are several good suggestions for silly proposals that worked.

$\mathscr{K}$athleen knew that Karl was going to propose on Christmas. There really wasn't much of a surprise in store for her. Determined to make his proposal memorable, Karl constructed a game for Kathleen to help build anticipation for the big question. He took the cardboard tubes from six rolls of toilet paper and in the center of each one he taped a Lifesaver. Then he stuffed the ends of each tube with tissue paper and wrapped his creations with festive paper and ribbons. He placed the rolls on a tray and told Kathleen that the ring was in the center of one of these gifts. She would be allowed to open one surprise package every ten minutes until she found the ring.

What Kathleen didn't know was that Karl had already placed the engagement ring in her bedroom under her pillow. As she opened the first gift and felt the Lifesaver inside, Kathleen's eyes lit up with excitement since she assumed that she had found the ring. Upon further examination, to her disappointment, the ring turned out to be a cherry-flavored Lifesaver. Ten minutes later she opened the next gift. Again a Lifesaver. On her final pick, after one hour of this game, Kathleen picked her sixth Lifesaver. Confused, she looked to Karl for an explanation.

"At night, where do you dream about spending our life together?" he asked.

Kathleen sprinted to her bedroom to find her ring under the pillow. She exclaimed with excitement, "This beats anything the tooth fairy ever left!"

❧

$\mathscr{M}$itch gave Claire a Raggedy Ann doll for her birthday. As she held the doll, Claire felt something hard and sharp beneath the bodice of the dress. Lifting the apron, she noticed a shiny diamond ring pinned to the sewn-in red heart on Raggedy Ann's chest. Claire gave Raggedy Ann a big hug, but it's Mitch who will always be the doll closest to Claire's heart!

✤

*J*amie's Sunday night ritual involved taking a bubblebath with her *People* magazine in hand. One Sunday evening, Randy was drawing a bath for her when he exclaimed, "Jamie, what is this ring in the bathtub?" Surprised to hear that the tub was dirty, she ran to look. Instead of finding a ring around the bathtub, Jamie discovered a sparkling engagement ring in the bathtub. Randy's prank made a real splash!

$\mathcal{L}$ IS FOR
LANDMARK PROPOSALS

Like the Eiffel Tower in Paris or the Space Needle in Seattle, like the Arch in St. Louis or the covered bridges in Madison County, there are well-known statues or monuments in most cities and towns. The best thing about getting engaged at a landmark is that your proposal will have a monumental impact forever after.

While Adam and Jennifer were on vacation in San Francisco, Adam orchestrated a classic landmark marriage proposal. *Breakfast at Tiffany's* was Jen's all-time favorite movie, so in the morning Adam took Jen to Tiffany & Company, where they window shopped and then shared croissants and coffee—much like Audrey Hepburn had done in the film classic. Then, Adam took Jen to San Francisco's most famous landmark, the Golden Gate Bridge. The two walked across the bridge, hand in hand, as the fog was burned away by the midday sun.

When they reached the center of the bridge, Adam asked the question Jen had been waiting to hear. Now this San Francisco landmark remains a symbol of their enduring love.

❧

The perfect spot for a landmark proposal in Maui is the island's famous dormant volcano, Mt. Haleakala. Jeff and Rena drove to the top of the volcano, 10,000 feet above sea level, to share a picnic and watch the sunset. As they neared the peak, Jeff noticed clouds beginning to form. The ominous weather did not dissuade him, though, and he persisted with his plan. When they reached their destination, the clouds had thickened and the air had turned cold. Rena wore a sun dress and Jeff was in shorts and sandals, *not* ideal attire for this unseasonable weather. The two huddled together for warmth and looked at each other in disbelief. How could it be so cold in Hawaii?

Jeff spotted a glassed-in shelter where they could observe the foggy view protected from the wind. Determined not to let his volcano-at-sunset plan be ruined by the cold, Jeff got down on one knee and pulled a ring out of his pocket. Rena accepted his proposal immediately, and the two raced back to the car to get out of the cold.

As they descended the volcano and emerged from the clouds, the weather improved and Rena spotted a perfect place for their picnic. The sun had just begun to set on the ocean below. They hurried to spread out the blanket so they could spend their first moments of being engaged as planned: on the volcano, sharing a picnic, and enjoying the sunset.

$\mathcal{M}$ IS FOR
MOVIE PROPOSALS

Many "An Affair to Remember" got its start in a darkened theater or on a cozy couch watching a romantic movie together.

$\mathcal{L}$auren and Brian made many trips to the video store in an attempt to rent *Sleepless in Seattle*, Lauren's favorite film. Unfortunately, every time they tried, they found that the movie was already rented. Inspired by her persistence, Brian came up with a great idea for a proposal. He decided to make a video of himself proposing to Lauren—complete with signs, visual aids, and costumes. Once the filming was done, Brian borrowed the tape jacket for *Sleepless in Seattle* from the video store and then he dashed off to his girlfriend's apartment with movie in hand and ring in pocket. Lauren, excited to see that Brian had finally found the film, quickly popped it into the VCR. She squealed with delight as the homemade video opened with her favorite song and revealed Brian's clever performance. On the video, Brian held up signs that read: "Will you marry me?" and "Just say yes!" In person, Brian got down on one knee and presented his future wife with an engagement ring. Of course Lauren said yes and now Brian is her permanent leading man.

❖

$\mathcal{S}$tacy and Josh had spent a tearful afternoon reading *The Bridges of Madison County* aloud to each other one rainy day. Naturally, when the movie opened they were among the first to see it. Just as the film's heroine, Francesca, falls in love with Robert Kincaid under the Rosemont Bridge, Josh removed a velvet ring box from his pocket and carefully placed it into the tub of popcorn he and Stacy were sharing. When Stacy reached into the bucket, she felt something odd and gasped in surprise. Josh fished the box out of the popcorn, opened it, and asked Stacy to be his "Francesca" forever.

❧

$\mathcal{J}$eff proposed to Renata with an original, cinematic flair. With the help of a friend who was a film school student, Jeff got to work editing and splicing his copy of *When Harry Met Sally.* The movie includes montages of older couples sitting on a couch and reflecting back on their many years of marital bliss. Jeff inserted himself into this scene costumed as an aged man, complete with gray hair, spectacles, cardigan, and pipe, and he reminisced about the past fifty years of happiness that he had shared with Renata. By fast-forwarding into their future, Jeff convinced Renata that her destiny was to be his mate for life.

$\mathcal{N}$ IS FOR
NO-HOLDS-BARRED PROPOSALS

The proposal in this chapter is the most elaborate, well-orchestrated event in this book. More than just a proposal, it's an award-winning happening.

$\mathscr{M}$ike and Kris had planned to meet at Kris's place one Thursday night for dinner. Nothing special. Nothing fancy. Just dinner together. Kris arrived home from work expecting to find Mike already there and dinner waiting. Instead of finding her boyfriend, however, she found three cassette tapes, a card, and a large, empty gift bag on the kitchen table. She picked up the card that said "READ THIS FIRST" and saw that it instructed her to take the bag and tapes to her car and listen to "Surprise Tape #1." And thus Kris's adventure began . . . .

Cassette #1 contained a mix of instructions from Mike directing Kris to various places and romantic music to listen to as she drove. The first direction sent Kris to her favorite local boutique. As she entered the store, the shopkeeper handed Kris a large wrapped box that she was told not to open but to place in the gift bag that Mike had provided. The next instruction sent Kris to the convenience store across town. There, too, Kris was presented with a wrapped box to be added to her collection of gifts.

Flipping the cassette to Side B, Kris learned that her next stop was at the drug store. Mike's voice directed her to see the pharmacist, who handed Kris yet another bag full of wrapped goodies. Then it was on to a liquor store, where the manager brought out a gaily wrapped bottle.

Surprise Tape #2 directed Kris first to a bookstore, where she picked up one more wrapped package, and then to a florist for another gift.

Finally, Mike's voice told Kris: "I was thinking of taking you on a picnic, or maybe to McDonalds, but I thought that wouldn't be special enough. So meet me at Washington Square restaurant, the place where we had our first date, and be sure to bring all the gifts you have collected."

At the restaurant a hostess showed Kris to a quiet table in the corner. There she found Mike, dressed in a tuxedo and holding a long florist box in his arms.

Before dinner Mike told Kris to open the gift she had picked up at the flower shop. Inside was a beautiful corsage that Mike pinned to her dress. After dinner, the happy couple exited the restaurant to find a white stretch limousine awaiting them. Mike told Kris to put the final tape into the stereo and their song, "Unchained Melody," played. Then Mike presented her with the long florist box. As she had suspected, the box contained a dozen red roses, but nestled among the flowers was a completely unexpected engagement ring. Mike got down on his knee in the limousine and proposed to Kris. She was so overwhelmed that he had to ask her three times before she responded, "Yes!"

Now, at last, Mike told Kris to open all the other gifts. The first was a beautiful outfit designed for a night on the town. The next box contained a deck of cards. Then came a bag with suntan lotion and chewing gum, followed by a bottle of champagne and an issue of *Bride's Magazine*. The last gift was a pair of tickets to Las Vegas, where Kris could use all her gifts during the fun-filled romantic weekend Mike had planned.

O IS FOR
ON-THE-JOB PROPOSALS

Consider an on-the-job proposal as an opportunity for promotion from your single state to happy couple status!

$\mathscr{L}$exi is a sales representative for a vineyard in Napa Valley, California. One miserable rainy day, just as Lexi was about to leave for home, her boss came up with a special request. He wanted Lexi to deliver an expensive bottle of wine to a very important client staying at the exclusive Auberge de Soleil. Reluctantly, Lexi took the wine and headed out into the storm.

When Lexi arrived at the hotel, she took the wine to the concierge, who instructed her to deliver it personally to the guest's room. As she headed for the room, Lexi began to feel nostalgic since this was the hotel where she and her boyfriend, George, had celebrated their two-year anniversary just a few months before. She reached the room she was looking for and knocked on the door. There was no answer. She tried the handle and the door opened. Inside, flames crackled in the fireplace and three dozen long-stemmed roses perfumed the air. One bloom in particular caught Lexi's eye, for it held a sparkling diamond ring in its center. As she entered and called out, "Hello!" her soon-to-be fiancé appeared. George welcomed Lexi with a kiss and asked her to be his wife. Then he took the ring from the flowers and placed it on Lexi's finger. They celebrated their engagement with a room-service banquet and a great wine. A toast to Lexi and George!

✦

$\mathcal{B}$rett worked as a law clerk for a judge. He invited his girlfriend, Melissa, and both their families to hear him present his judge's opinion for public record. Brett explained to Melissa that this was an exciting event, for he was the first clerk ever selected to speak on behalf of a judge.

Both families gathered in the courtroom for Brett's motion. The three-judge panel, clad in black robes and seated on an elevated oak dais, began the proceedings. "We call this court to order. Mr. Ingerman, please begin your motion to the court."

Brett began, "May I respectfully request permission to have Ms. Talles join me at the council's table?" The judges granted Brett's request, and Melissa came forward.

"Before I begin my motion, I would like to introduce Ms. Talles to the court." Brett chronicled their relationship in a two-minute monologue and declared his love for Melissa using formal legal terminology. She blushed in embarrassment, thinking that Brett was exceeding the boundaries of decorum. He concluded, "Therefore, before this court and with this court's permission, I would like to go on record asserting the following proposition: Melissa Talles, will you marry me?" Melissa whispered "Yes" and the judges voted unanimous approval.

Brett's judge even issued an opinion from the bench, which read:

> *Brett proposed to Melissa and she said yes.*
> *Seeing that the parties have acted reasonably and*
> *in good faith, we affirm this as a final judgment.*

$\mathcal{P}$ IS FOR
PICNIC PROPOSALS

If you get off to a good start, life together can be a picnic!

$\mathcal{L}$arry planned the ultimate picnic. He packed a basket with wine and cheese and other tasty surprises and whisked Debbie off into the countryside. After a relaxing lunch on a red-and-white-checked blanket, it was time to indulge in dessert. Larry had bought Debbie's favorite: carrot cake. Debbie savored her first taste of moist cake and cream cheese frosting. On her next bite, though, her fork collided with a different kind of carrot: a two-carat diamond engagement ring!

❧

$\mathscr{G}$iovanni had planned a gourmet Italian picnic complete with pasta salads, Chianti, and focaccia. He hired a limousine and picked out the perfect spot where he and Tina could share their picnic lunch high on a cliff overlooking the ocean. As they neared the site, however, the sky grew dark and rain poured down on the scene. Not to be deterred by the unexpected shower, Giovanni simply switched to Plan B. He spread the picnic blanket in the back of the limo, set up for their feast, and handed the driver a list of places that had been important to both Tina and him in their relationship. They drove by their favorite coffee house, the park where they first kissed, and the field where they played co-ed softball on many a weekend. The tour of these significant, romantic spots accompanied by the Italian picnic spread set the stage for this rained-out picnic proposal. With their favorite opera, "La Traviata," playing in the background, Giovanni asked Tina to marry him. She responded, "Of course!" and brightened up that rainy day!

$\mathcal{Q}$ IS FOR
QUIRKY PROPOSALS

Some people add more than just a little twist to their proposals, as in the unusual stories that follow.

$\mathscr{K}$elly and Denise were avid horseback riders, so Kelly decided to plan an unforgettable equestrian proposal. He invited Denise to meet him at the stables for an afternoon ride. When she arrived, she saw a most unusual sight. There in the ring was a lone rider in a full suit of armor astride a beautiful white stallion. The stranger motioned for Denise to join him in the ring. When she hesitated, he raised his faceplate and Denise immediately recognized the knight in shining armor as Kelly. She drew closer to Kelly and he reached down to swoop her up onto the horse. Once she was settled, Kelly signaled the horse to take them away. As they rode through the woods, the handsome knight asked the beautiful damsel to be his lady for life. Now that's a novel way to get hitched!

❖

*N*othing could be more quirky than Steve's proposal to Jenny. He recruited all his friends and relatives to play the role of spies in his quest for his true love. The proposal involved an elaborate plan, which required each spy to meet Jenny at a designated location at a particular time. Each participant was essential to the plan, and all spies were encouraged to dress the part (i.e., sunglasses, trench coats, or funny hats to disguise themselves).

When Jenny arrived home after work, she found a note that read:

The time has come for me to make a confession that may rock your world. I am not really a mild-mannered attorney with a passion for volleyball and infused oil recipes. I am a secret agent in the service of King John of Allisee. The King is on his deathbed and the rite of succession can only occur if we recover his long-lost treasure. Without the treasure, when the King dies, my homeland will fall into the hands of a gang of evil thugs. I need your help in

retrieving the King's treasure. The gang is hot on my trail, and although my years of martial arts training and superior physical condition give me an edge, it may not be enough. Clues are placed around the apartment that may help you find me.
GODSPEED

Following this dramatic introduction were creative clues that instructed Jenny on what to do and where to go. She found one clue in a candle embedded in wax, another in the Boggle™ word game, and yet another in a plastic bag tucked into her bubble bath bottle! Movie tickets led her to a nearby theater, where a driver clad in black handed Jenny a box of Milk Duds that contained the next clue. The driver took her to the monkey house of the local zoo, where another spy was waiting to hand her a membership card to the aquarium and a fishing pole. From the aquarium Jenny was sent to the beach and from the beach to a fancy downtown restaurant. At the restaurant the waiter handed her the final clue, which read:

> *Whoever among you is most strong of body, agile of wit, and wise beyond her years shall be my successor. She must possess judgment, character and beauty. Most importantly, my trusted counselor Steve must deem her "okay." If any such person can be found by midnight of this day, she must be offered my treasure. If she accepts the throne, she will accept the treasure of the kingdom. Good luck and Godspeed.*

Engagement ring in hand, Steve appeared and said to Jenny, "You are the only person who fits the King's description. Will you accept his treasure?" She did, of course, and the two still reign in their Kingdom of Love.

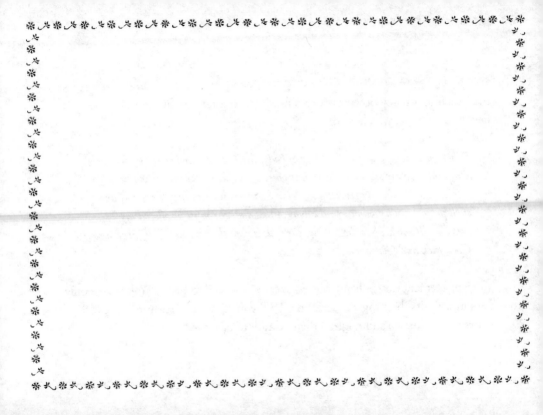

$\mathcal{R}$ IS FOR
ROMANTIC PROPOSALS

"Cupid, draw back your bow, and let your arrow go straight to my lover's heart . . ."

$\mathscr{B}$rett combined the knight-in-shining-armor theme with a scavenger hunt for Jenn. He hid small gifts all around their apartment and provided written clues to the whereabouts of each one. Jenn collected flowers, chocolate kisses, a bottle of champagne, a teddy bear, and a ten-dollar gift certificate for a manicure before she was instructed to meet her prince at the Miami Beach Convention Center gardens. Brett greeted her, clad in a rented suit of armor, and on one knee he gallantly declared his love and asked for her hand in marriage. Jenn accepted and headed straight to the manicurist to groom her hands so she could show off her new ring! She dubbed this evening a knight to remember!

❖

Dan proposed to Samantha during a Fourth of July fireworks extravaganza. The lovers sat, holding hands and cuddling together as they watched the dazzling display. As the grand finale began and the entire sky was aflame, Dan proposed to her: "Samantha, you bring such sparkle and joy into my life that I burn inside when I think of you. I love you so. Will you marry me and be my happily ever after?" Shocked and thrilled, Samantha threw her arms around Dan and as they kissed, both truly saw sky rockets.

$\mathcal{K}$aty and Andrew had a weekend getaway planned at a bed-and-breakfast country inn. While Katy was soaking in a relaxing bubblebath, Andrew filled the room with flowers. On their bed, he arranged rose petals to spell "Will you marry me?" When Katy emerged from the bathroom, she stopped to smell the roses and accepted his proposal.

$\mathcal{S}$ IS FOR
SECOND-TIME-AROUND PROPOSALS

Even if your first shot at marriage missed the mark, the second one may be the one that's right on target.

The day after her divorce was final, Glenn called Jill and asked her on a date. They spent a wonderful day on the Boardwalk riding the merry-go-round, floating through the Tunnel of Love, and eating cotton candy. Glenn even presented Jill with a cuddly teddy bear he won at a carnival game. At the end of the day, Glenn said to Jill, "I am going to marry you."

"Oh no you're not!" she replied. "I am never getting married again."

Their relationship evolved, and after two years of getting to know one another better, Glenn was ready to pop the question. Jill kept the teddy bear from their first date on her bed, and one night as she pulled back the covers she noticed a ring tied around the neck of the stuffed animal. A note was attached that read: "If you accept this invitation to be my wife, meet me at noon tomorrow on the Boardwalk, next to the *marry*-go-round." She did—and their meeting turned out to be a "merry" occasion.

$\mathcal{S}$tan and his two daughters were at the park one Saturday with Kristen, his long-time girlfriend. There definitely was a feeling of family that day as the kids played on the swings while Kristen and Stan set up for a picnic. When Stan headed off to call the girls to lunch, Kristen watched the three of them and felt happy to be part of this group. The girls giggled as they neared the picnic table, each holding tightly to their father's hands.

"The girls and I have something to ask you, Kris," Stan said.

"Okay," she answered.

"The girls want to ask first," Stan prompted.

"Will you be our new mommy?" they chimed in unison.

Kristen was surprised and a bit confused.

Stan followed, "We would all like you to be my wife. Will you join our family?"

Kristen was so touched that they had all asked her together. How special that her new daughters and future husband all participated in this proposal.

"Of course I'll be your new mommy and wife!" she exclaimed. The four of them hugged tightly and settled into their first lunch as an engaged family.

$\mathcal{T}$ IS FOR TV PROPOSALS

On the tube or in front of it, TV proposals can be a hit with the right audience.

$\mathscr{E}$ven Steven Spielberg couldn't have done it better than Andy when he wrote, produced, and starred in his own television commercial to propose to Dionne. On Dionne's birthday, which also happened to be Christmas Eve, Andy purchased air time on the Lifetime Channel. Friends and family gathered around the TV and watched in amazement as Andy appeared on the screen.

He began with a hook, "Hey, Dionne! Wouldn't it be nice to come home to something other than an empty apartment every day?"

Then he went into a snappy sales pitch, "Say yes and you'll receive countless years of laughter, thoughtfulness, devotion, spontaneity, and, of course, fantastic sex!"

As he delivered his lines, various images of their future life together flashed across the screen. There was Andy doing dishes and bringing Dionne breakfast in bed. In the final scene, Andy walked towards the camera, got down on one knee, took a ring out of his shirt pocket and asked, "If you're ready, Di, will you be my wife?"

Then he turned to his girlfriend in person and placed the ring on her finger. When Dionne said "Yes," Andy counted his production a commercial success!

❧

$\mathcal{T}$om and Theresa have a passion for Chinese food. In fact, every Monday night they order in a Chinese dinner and settle down in front of the TV to watch their favorite nighttime soap together. Tom used the occasion of a TV wedding ceremony to surprise Theresa with a novel proposal. He raced to the door when dinner arrived and whisked the meal into the kitchen, where he inserted his own message into the fortune cookies. When Theresa opened her cookie she read: "If Billy and Brooke can do it, why can't we?" Fortunately she replied, "We can!"

$\mathcal{U}$ IS FOR
UNDERWATER PROPOSALS

It doesn't have to be 20,000 Leagues Under the Sea *to be an ideal setting for romance. You can swim, snorkel, or scuba your way into the future together.*

$\mathcal{L}$eslie has her Ph.D. in Marine Geology and is an avid scuba diver. Much of her free time and her entire career are devoted to the ocean. She and Cameron, her boyfriend, planned a relaxing get-away vacation in Mexico, and, of course, scuba diving was high on their agenda of activities. On a dive one morning, Leslie came upon an oyster shell sitting atop a coral reef. Leslie knew that this sea life was definitely out of place in Acapulco waters. Curious, she picked up the shell to examine it. (Little did she know that her boyfriend had planted it there just moments earlier!) Cameron reached for the oyster and whipped out his dive knife. He started jabbing at the shell to open it. Leslie protested with underwater pantomime in her best "save the marine life" attitude, but Cameron went ahead and handed her the half-open oyster. To her surprise, instead of finding a pearl, she found a "diamond" ring inside this oyster. (Leslie later learned that it was a fake ring as Cameron wisely decided to give her the real ring on dry land.) Cameron slipped the ring on Leslie's finger and wrote on his dive slate, "Okay?" She wrote back, "You're crazy, but I love you!" These two were ready to take the plunge!

❦

*A*manda and Paul were on a dive exploring a sunken ship. Inside the ship, Paul stumbled upon an old, rusted treasure chest covered with barnacles. Amanda paddled over and helped Paul pry it open. To her delight, the chest contained coins and pearls and what looked like a genie's lamp. In the center of the chest, attached to a fishing line, was a sparkling gum-ball-machine engagement ring. "Will you marry me?" Paul mouthed as he placed the ring on her finger. Amanda smiled and enthusiastically nodded, "Yes." Some people will go to any depths to make a proposal memorable.

P.S. Beware! *Another less fortunate groom-to-be dropped a diamond ring while under water. For safety's sake, go for a fake ring under water and keep the real one back on dry land.*

$\mathscr{V}$ IS FOR
VACATION
PROPOSALS

What could be more memorable than a vacation that begins a lifetime together?

$\mathscr{B}$arbara and Rick were vacationing in Disneyland to celebrate her birthday. After a day of exciting rides and shows and plenty of corn dogs and popcorn, the two settled on the curbside to watch the nightly Electric Light Parade. Tiny white lights twinkled in the trees as the Disneyland characters danced their way down Main Street. The seven dwarfs marched by with Snow White, and Cinderella waved from her pumpkin coach. Then Mickey and Minnie Mouse drove up on their float. As they neared Barbara and Rick, Mickey got down on one knee and took out a huge paper maché diamond ring to give to his mousy gal. Rick followed his lead and, similarly, kneeled to propose to Barbara. Rick's animated vacation proposal had a storybook ending.

❧

$\mathcal{S}$eth and Cori were on vacation in Aspen, Colorado, hiking up the Ute Trail. This strenuous climb culminated at a rocky peak that overlooked the town of Aspen far below. Seth huffed and puffed his way up the mountain as Cori energetically took the lead. He gained on her as they neared the top, and the two were hand in hand as they reached the peak. Perched on a ledge atop the summit, Cori noticed a beautifully painted sign that read:

> *C.M.:*
> *Let's climb the peaks together.*
> *Say you will.*
> *I will love you forever.*
> *—S.P.B.*

She began to cry as Seth pulled a ring out of his fanny pack and said, "Be my wife. Be my best friend. I love you." Hikers nearby cheered the couple. Needless to say, this would be a vacation they'll never forget.

$\mathcal{W}$ IS FOR
WOMEN'S PROPOSALS TO MEN

You don't have to wait for Sadie Hawkins Day to grab your partner and go for it!

$\mathcal{A}$my and Todd met at law school, and three years later each was working at a different prestigious law firm. Although they had been dating for four years and had talked of marriage several times, Todd just couldn't seem to get up the nerve to ask Amy to be his wife. Finally, Amy decided to take matters into her own hands. She drafted a legal summons and had it delivered by a process server to Todd's office. The summons read:

> *I hereby declare my love to you as your partner and associate. No case is too difficult for us to win together. I subpoena you for life. Please sign this document in the presence of two legally competent witnesses and have it properly notarized. Your compliance will declare us officially engaged.*
>
> *I love you. Amy E. Johnson, Esq.*

Todd signed, of course, and the two became legal partners for life.

$\mathscr{G}$ail and Phillip had been together for over a year. They both knew that one day they would marry, but so far no one had asked the fateful question. One evening after a romantic candlelit dinner, the couple sat, arms entwined, on the sofa, sipping cognac. Phillip had just lit an expensive cigar when Gail turned to him and said: "You've stolen my heart, Phillip. Please take good care of it. I love you now and forever, so let's not lose any more 'time' before committing for life. Will you marry me and be my husband?"

Phillip was delighted. As a token of their engagement, Gail gave Phillip a watch. Phillip, not to be outdone, promptly took the paper ring off his cigar and placed it on Gail's finger, promising to replace it with a real engagement ring the very next day. Gail was glad that she took the initiative and got this relationship ticking along happily.

$\mathscr{X}$ IS FOR
X-RATED PROPOSALS

Add some sizzle to your offer and don't be afraid to get an X-rating on your proposition.

$\mathscr{K}$endra accompanied her boyfriend Jordan on what she thought to be a business trip. The two arrived at the airport, and a chauffeur ushered them to the private company plane. When Kendra climbed aboard, she noticed that the aircraft was particularly cozy. It was so private and romantic, in fact, that the cabin featured a heart-shaped bed. There were roses everywhere, and a bottle of fine champagne chilled in the silver cooler. Music played softly in the background.

"What kind of company plane is this?" Kendra asked.

"Actually, honey, this isn't quite the company plane. I rented this plane just for us, so that we could become members of the mile-high club," Jordan explained.

Kendra blushed. The pilot told them that they would be flying for three hours and they had only to buzz if they needed anything at all.

After takeoff, Jordan took a ring out of his briefcase and asked Kendra for her hand in marriage. Their engagement began with their entry into the mile-high club, and flying together was never quite the same after Jordan's indecent proposal!

On Valentine's Day, Nancy and Ben sat in the hot tub and gazed at the star-filled sky from the private patio of their hotel room in Lake Tahoe. One thing led to another and their relaxing soak steamed up to become a sexy skinny dip. Ben took advantage of the excitement of the moment to ask Nancy to be his playmate for life. He placed a ring on the finger of his longtime lover, and things have gone swimmingly for this couple ever since.

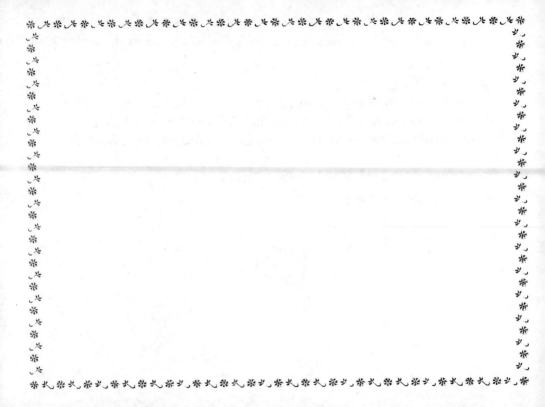

$\mathcal{Y}$ IS FOR
YUPPIE PROPOSALS

A small investment of time and effort in preparing a proposal can yield big dividends in terms of lifetime happiness.

$\mathcal{T}$iffany and Cliff had plans to meet at the local hot spot for a power lunch. Arriving late, Tiffany learned from the maître d' that Cliff was not yet there. She proceeded to the table and called Cliff at the office on her cellular phone. No luck. She then tried him on his portable phone. It wasn't on. Finally, she called his car phone and Cliff answered.

"I'm sorry, darling. I got caught up at a meeting with my stock broker. I'll be there as soon as I can."

When Cliff arrived, they ordered; just as lunch was being served, his cellular phone rang. Cliff answered and spoke animatedly with his broker. When he hung up, he exclaimed, "You'll never guess, Tif. The WYMM stock is really taking off. It is a sure-fire investment that guarantees many years of growth and prosperity." Cliff pulled from his briefcase the stock prospectus and continued, "I know you aren't a big investor, but I think you may want to consider this deal."

Tiffany nonchalantly glanced at the charts and graphs that covered the pages.

"Whatever you think, dear. How much should I invest?" she asked. Cliff urged her to read the information more carefully before deciding how many shares she would buy. When she focused on the prospectus, it read:

> *The* WYMM *stock is a sure thing. Your investment will last a lifetime and provides growth and great interest. If you decide to invest, your shares will yield high profits. The* WYMM *stock is another way of saying <u>Will You Marry Me</u>? Just say yes, Tiffany!*

Tiffany said, "Yes," and this merger shows signs of becoming a very profitable joint venture certain to last a lifetime.

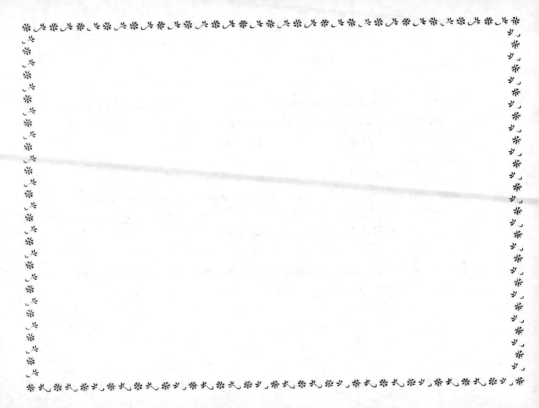

$\mathcal{Z}$ IS FOR
ZANY PROPOSALS

If you are crazy for each other, then a bizarre plan may be just what you need to pop the question.

$\mathscr{N}$eil's uncle had a friend in the police force who agreed to help out in this zany proposal. Neil bought Jacque concert tickets to celebrate their two-year anniversary. Jacque, as usual, was running late, and Neil had to hurry if they were to make the opening act of the concert. As he zoomed down the highway, he heard a siren and saw a red light flashing in his rear view mirror. Jacque felt terrible, thinking it was all her fault that Neil was being pulled over.

The highway patrol officer approached the window and began to question Neil harshly on the reason for his speeding. When Neil fumbled for answers, the officer forced him to take a sobriety test and then stated that he would have to take both of them in for questioning. Jacque was shocked. The police officer came to her side of the car and took out his handcuffs. Confused and frightened, Jacque began to cry. Her tears appeared to affect the officer, for suddenly he relented and said that there was one way he would let them off without a ticket.

"What is it?" Jacque asked.

The officer turned to Neil and said, "A man always needs a good woman to steer him in the right direction." That was Neil's cue.

"Jacque, will you take me into custody for life?" asked Neil.

Jacque was speechless and dazed. The officer put away the handcuffs and Neil cleared up the confusion when he got down on one knee and repeated, "Will you take me into custody for the rest of your life?"

Jacque found her voice in time to say "Yes!" and thus began Neil and Jacque's journey down the highway of life.

$\mathcal{D}$ean lived in Atlanta and Marcy lived in Los Angeles. For Valentine's Day, the couple decided to meet in Chicago, the halfway point in their cross-country courtship. Dean, however, took a roundabout route and first flew to Los Angeles so that he could accompany Marcy to Chicago incognito. Marcy got on the plane and took her seat. Shortly thereafter, someone sat down next to her. Marcy looked up to see a man wearing a turban and wrapped in fabric from head to toe, with only his eyes showing.

"Oh no," Marcy thought, "I'm stuck on a four-hour flight next to a real weirdo."

After takeoff, the flight attendant handed Marcy a telegram that she said had been delivered to the airport. Surprised, Marcy opened the envelope and found a truly romantic declaration of Dean's love for her. The man next to her kept glancing over, which annoyed Marcy during this very private moment. Tears of happiness welled in her eyes and suddenly, through the tears, she noticed that the man next to her was unwrapping his clothing. To her surprise, it was Dean! He had wanted to see her reaction to his words of love. The flight attendant promptly arrived with champagne, and Dean presented Marcy with a shiny engagement ring. "Will you be my Valentine for life?" he asked. Now that's a first-class zany proposal!

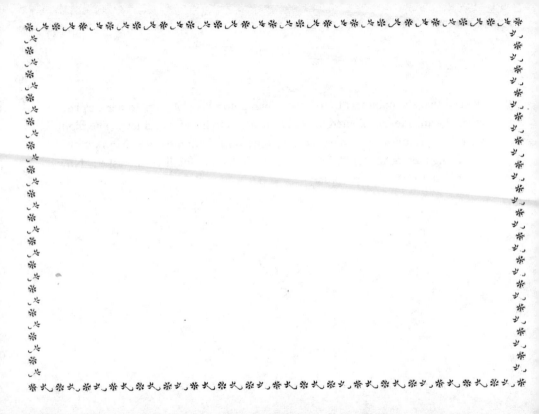

Concluding Remarks

I hope that you have been inspired by the clever, romantic proposals in this book. You can use these stories to help plan your own perfect moment. Remember, there is no right or wrong way to propose. Just be sure to mix in a little romance and a lot of love and you too can create a storybook proposal that you'll enjoy telling and retelling for many years to come. Let your own imagination provide the ideal beginning for your happily ever after. Good luck and happy proposing!!!

Photo by Eliot Holtzman

About the Author

Cynthia Clumeck Muchnick was born and raised in Marin County, California. She pursued her undergraduate degree in Art History and Political Science at Stanford University where she met met her future husband, Adam Muchnick. After completing college, Cindy moved to Chicago to begin her career in college admissions while Adam attended law school. One spring break, the two were on vacation in Paris when Adam popped the fateful question and sparked Cindy's interest in collecting marriage proposals and writing *Will You Marry Me?*

Cindy and Adam now live happily ever after in Orange County, California.

SEND ME YOUR MARRIAGE PROPOSALS!

If the stories in this book have inspired you or if you or someone you know has planned and executed a romantic proposal, we want to know about it. Please send a copy of the story on cassette or in writing to:

Marriage Proposals
ARCO
1633 Broadway
New York, NY   10019

Be sure to include your name, address, and phone number with the story so that you can be contacted if yours is chosen for my sequel, *More of the World's Most Romantic Proposals from A to Z.*

Acknowledgments

Will You Marry Me? could not have been a success without the dedication, love, and support of many people:

• My boundless gratitude to all the couples too numerous to list who shared their engagement stories with me in person and by phone, fax, and the mail. Your loving anecdotes attest that romance, chivalry, and creativity are alive and well in the world.

• Special thanks to Karen and Benjamin, Linda, Alan, and Lauren, Marc and Kim, Grandma Lois, Adam and Jen, my in-house legal team, Adam and Cheryl for their neighborly fax services, Scott Stoddart, all of my friends, and Stanford University for providing the ideal setting in the Rodin Sculpture Garden for my first kiss with Adam where this adventure all began.

• To Linda Bernbach, my editor at Macmillan, thank you for putting up with my barrage of phone calls and abundant enthusiasm for this project. Your friendly and patient demeanor always assured me that you really cared. To all of the people in marketing and promotions who helped out, thank you for your dedication to this engaging project.

• To my new family, the Muchnicks, who spent many a lunch date working on puns and the humor element of my book. Thank you for your endless encouragement and for being such wonderful parents to my husband and now to me.

• Mom and Dad, you both taught me to make lemonade out of lemons and to savor each passing moment. I dared to fail gloriously and it was well worth it. Your continuous support, love, and encouragement assure me that you will always believe in me.

• And, finally, to my loving husband, Adam, who stands beside me in everything I do and who gave me the inspiration to write this book. You are my best friend, lover, teammate, cheerleader, coach, fan, confidante, and other half. I love you.

—*Cynthia Clumeck Muchnick*